I0021683

Table of contents

Bonus included

FOCUS on Trading skills : Improve your crypto trading process

Foreword

Welcome to the dynamic and ever-evolving world of cryptocurrencies. In this guide, "Improve Your Crypto Skills," we delve into the intricate and multifaceted realm of digital currencies, a domain that continues to captivate the imagination and interest of people around the globe.

Cryptocurrencies, since their inception with the launch of Bitcoin in 2009, have not only challenged our traditional notions of money but have also opened doors to new and innovative financial ecosystems. They represent more than just a digital form of currency; they are a testament to the power of decentralized technology and the potential for creating a more inclusive financial system.

This guide is designed for individuals who are enthralled by the potential of cryptocurrencies and are eager to deepen their understanding and proficiency. Whether you are a novice just starting out on your crypto journey or an experienced trader looking to refine your skills, this book offers valuable insights and practical advice.

We will explore the foundational concepts of blockchain technology, demystify the mechanics of various cryptocurrencies, and provide you with the tools to analyze and navigate the market effectively. From understanding the nuances of trading and investment strategies to grasping the complexities of smart contracts and the exciting world of DeFi (Decentralized Finance), our aim is to equip you with the knowledge and skills necessary to thrive in this rapidly changing landscape.

As we embark on this journey together, remember that the world of cryptocurrencies is not just about making profitable trades or investments; it's about being part of a revolutionary movement that is reshaping the future of finance. So, let's turn the page and begin this exciting adventure in the world of cryptocurrencies, where learning and growth await at every turn.

Introduction

In the realm of finance and investment, cryptocurrencies have emerged as a revolutionary force, offering a unique blend of technology and monetary potential. This digital asset class, characterized by its decentralized nature and reliance on blockchain technology, has not just captured the imagination of the tech-savvy but has also opened new avenues for wealth creation. As individuals across the globe seek to understand and leverage these digital currencies, the question "How can one become rich with cryptocurrencies?" becomes increasingly pertinent.

Understanding the Cryptocurrency Landscape

The journey to wealth through cryptocurrencies begins with understanding what they are and how they work. Cryptocurrencies are digital or virtual currencies secured by cryptography, making them nearly immune to counterfeiting or double-spending. They are decentralized networks based on blockchain technology—a distributed ledger enforced by a disparate network of computers. This decentralization offers freedom from traditional banking systems and governmental control.

Bitcoin, created by an anonymous entity named Satoshi Nakamoto in 2009, was the first cryptocurrency and remains the most well-known and valuable. Since then, thousands of alternative cryptocurrencies with various features and specifications have been developed, including Ethereum, Ripple, Litecoin, and more. These digital assets have introduced concepts like smart contracts, decentralized finance (DeFi), and Non-Fungible Tokens (NFTs), further expanding the scope of the crypto ecosystem.

Early Adoption and Historical Growth

The initial surge in cryptocurrency popularity came from its promise of substantial returns. Early adopters of Bitcoin, who invested when it was a fraction of its current value, have seen exponential growth in their investments. This historical growth has been a key driving factor in attracting new investors, although it's important to acknowledge that the crypto market is highly volatile and past performance is not indicative of future results.

Investment Strategies in Cryptocurrency

Becoming rich through cryptocurrencies is not guaranteed, but certain strategies have proven effective for some investors. These include:

1. **Long-Term Holding (HODLing):** This strategy involves buying cryptocurrencies and holding onto them for an extended period, regardless of market volatility. It is based on the belief that despite short-term fluctuations, the value of well-chosen cryptocurrencies will increase significantly over the long term.

2. **Active Trading:** Unlike HODLing, active trading involves buying and selling cryptocurrencies over shorter periods, capitalizing on market trends and fluctuations. It requires a good understanding of the market, analytical skills, and often, access to trading tools and algorithms.

3. **Diversification:** Just as with traditional investing, diversification is crucial in the crypto market. Investing in a variety of cryptocurrencies can reduce risk, as the performance

of different coins can vary widely.

4. **Initial Coin Offerings (ICOs) and Token Sales:** Investing in ICOs or token sales can be a way to get in early on a new cryptocurrency. However, this comes with high risk as many ICOs have failed or turned out to be scams.

Risk Management and Research

The volatile nature of cryptocurrencies makes risk management essential. This includes only investing money one can afford to lose, setting clear goals, and having an exit strategy. Moreover, thorough research is vital. Understanding the technology behind cryptocurrencies, staying updated with market trends, and being aware of regulatory changes are crucial aspects of informed investing.

Staying Informed and Adapting to Changes

The cryptocurrency market is rapidly evolving, with new technologies, regulations, and market dynamics emerging regularly. Staying informed through credible sources, participating in community discussions, and continuous learning are key to adapting to these changes.

Legal and Ethical Considerations

It's also important to consider legal and ethical aspects. Compliance with tax laws and regulations in one's jurisdiction is essential. Furthermore, the ethical implications of investing in cryptocurrencies, considering their environmental impact and association with illicit activities, should be considered.

Conclusion

In conclusion, while there is no guaranteed path to becoming rich with cryptocurrencies, understanding the market, employing effective strategies, managing risks, and staying informed are crucial steps toward potential financial success. As with any investment, it's important to approach cryptocurrency with caution, knowledge, and a clear strategy. The digital gold rush is fraught with challenges and opportunities, and navigating it successfully requires a blend of wisdom, patience, and adaptability.

Chapter 1

Blockchain Protocol : Comprehensive guide

In the digital era, blockchain technology has emerged as a groundbreaking innovation, reshaping how data is stored, transactions are conducted, and trust is established in a decentralized manner. At the heart of this transformative technology is the blockchain protocol, a complex yet fascinating system that underpins cryptocurrencies like Bitcoin and Ethereum, as well as a myriad of other applications beyond the realm of digital currencies. This guide aims to provide a comprehensive understanding of blockchain protocol, its components, functioning, and implications in various sectors.

Understanding Blockchain Protocol

A blockchain protocol is essentially a set of rules that govern how data is recorded, shared, and maintained on a blockchain network. It's a shared, immutable ledger that facilitates the process of recording transactions and tracking assets in a business network. The protocol ensures security, transparency, and decentralization, making it a powerful tool for various applications.

Key Components of Blockchain Protocol

1. **Data Structure:** The data on a blockchain is grouped into blocks, each containing a list of transactions. Every block is linked to the previous one through a cryptographic hash, forming a chain, hence the name 'blockchain'.

2. **Consensus Mechanism:** This is the process used to achieve agreement on a single data value among distributed processes or systems. Popular mechanisms include Proof of Work (PoW) and Proof of Stake (PoS).

3. **Decentralization:** Unlike traditional databases, blockchains are typically decentralized, meaning they aren't controlled by a single entity. This is achieved through a network of nodes, each participating in the consensus process.

4. **Cryptography:** Cryptography ensures the security of the transactions and maintains the integrity of the blockchain. Public-key cryptography is used for secure identity verification.

5. **Smart Contracts:** These are self-executing contracts with the terms of the agreement between buyer and seller being directly written into lines of code, automating and enforcing contract terms.

How Blockchain Protocol Works

1. **Transaction Initiation:** A user initiates a transaction, which could be a cryptocurrency transfer, a data exchange, etc.

2. **Block Creation:** Once a transaction is initiated, it is grouped with other pending transactions to create a new block.

3. **Verification and Validation:** Nodes in the network verify the transactions in the block. In PoW, for instance, miners solve complex mathematical puzzles to validate transactions.

4. **Adding to the Chain:** Once validated, the new block is added to the blockchain, and

the transaction is complete. The new block contains a cryptographic hash of the previous block, creating a chain.

5. **Updating Nodes:** Every node in the network updates its copy of the blockchain ledger, maintaining consistency and transparency.

Applications of Blockchain Protocol

1. **Cryptocurrencies:** The most prominent application of blockchain protocols is in cryptocurrencies, digital or virtual currencies that use cryptography for security.

2. **Finance:** Blockchain is revolutionizing the financial industry by enabling faster, cheaper, and more secure transactions.

3. **Supply Chain Management:** Blockchain enhances transparency and traceability in supply chains, allowing for more efficient and reliable tracking of goods and services.

4. **Healthcare:** Securely storing and sharing patient data, and managing supply chains for medicines.

5. **Voting Systems:** Blockchain can provide secure and transparent digital voting systems, minimizing fraud and manipulation.

6. **Real Estate:** Streamlining property transactions and record-keeping, reducing fraud, and improving efficiency.

Challenges and Limitations

1. **Scalability:** As the number of transactions grows, the size of the blockchain increases, leading to scalability issues.

2. **Energy Consumption:** Protocols like PoW are energy-intensive, raising environmental concerns.

3. **Regulatory Challenges:** The decentralized nature of blockchain makes it challenging to fit within traditional regulatory frameworks.

4. **Security Concerns:** While secure, blockchains are not immune to attacks, such as the 51% attack in PoW networks.

5. **Adoption Barriers:** The complexity and novelty of the technology can be barriers to widespread adoption.

The Future of Blockchain Protocol

The future of blockchain protocol is incredibly promising, with ongoing research and development aimed at overcoming its current limitations. Innovations like layer-2 solutions, alternative consensus mechanisms, and interoperability advancements are paving the way for more efficient, sustainable, and user-friendly blockchain systems.

Blockchain's potential to create more transparent, secure, and equitable systems across various sectors is immense. From finance to healthcare, supply chain to governance, the implications of this technology are far-reaching, promising to redefine how we interact with the digital world.

Conclusion

In conclusion, the blockchain protocol represents a paradigm shift in how information is recorded and shared. Its principles of decentralization, transparency, and security offer a new framework for digital interactions.

Chapter 2
The essentials of Bitcoin Mining

Bitcoin mining is the process by which new bitcoins are entered into circulation and is a crucial component of the maintenance and development of the blockchain ledger. This guide provides a comprehensive overview of Bitcoin mining, including its workings, necessary equipment, and considerations for those interested in engaging in this unique digital endeavor.

Understanding Bitcoin Mining

Bitcoin mining involves solving complex mathematical problems using computer hardware. Miners compete to solve these problems; the first to solve it adds a new block of transactions to the blockchain and is rewarded with bitcoins. This process not only introduces new bitcoins into the system but also secures the network and verifies transactions.

The Mining Process

1. **Transaction Verification:** Miners verify transactions to ensure their legitimacy. These transactions are gathered into a memory pool or 'mempool'.

2. **Forming a Block:** Once enough transactions are gathered, miners attempt to form a block.

3. **Solving the Puzzle:** Miners use computational power to solve a cryptographic puzzle, which requires generating a hash that is lower than or equal to the target hash set by the network.

4. **Adding to the Blockchain:** When a miner successfully solves the puzzle, they broadcast the block to the network for validation. Other miners verify the solution, and the block is added to the blockchain.

5. **Receiving Rewards:** The successful miner receives a block reward in bitcoins (which halves approximately every four years) and transaction fees.

Equipment Needed for Bitcoin Mining

1. **Mining Hardware:** Early days of Bitcoin allowed mining using regular PCs. However, now, specialized hardware like ASIC (Application-Specific Integrated Circuit) miners are required for efficiency.

2. **Mining Software:** Software connects your hardware to the blockchain and Bitcoin mining pool if you're part of one.

3. **Electricity and Cooling Systems:** Mining consumes a lot of electricity and generates heat, necessitating efficient cooling systems.

4. **Internet Connection:** A stable and fast internet connection is essential for continuous mining operations.

Choosing a Mining Method

1. **Solo Mining:** This is where a miner performs the mining operations alone. While the rewards are not shared, the chances of solving a block on your own are meager.

2. **Mining Pools:** These are groups of miners who combine their computational power to increase their chances of mining a block. Rewards are shared proportionally to the

contributed processing power.

3. **Cloud Mining:** This involves renting mining power from a company which owns large mining farms. It's a way to mine without managing hardware but comes with risks and lower profits.

Understanding Mining Difficulty

Mining difficulty, a measure of how hard it is to find a hash below the target, adjusts approximately every two weeks to ensure that a block is found every 10 minutes on average. As more miners join the network and as mining technology advances, the difficulty increases.

Legal and Regulatory Considerations

Bitcoin mining's legal status varies by country, with some governments welcoming it and others imposing strict regulations or outright bans. It's crucial to understand and comply with the laws and regulations in your region.

Economic Considerations

1. **Profitability:** This depends on factors like the price of Bitcoin, electricity costs, mining difficulty, and the initial investment in mining equipment.

2. **Bitcoin Halving:** Approximately every four years, the block reward halves, affecting profitability.

Environmental Impact

Bitcoin mining is energy-intensive and has raised concerns about its environmental impact. The growing emphasis on sustainable energy sources in mining operations is a step towards addressing these concerns.

The Future of Bitcoin Mining

Advancements in technology, changes in regulations, and the evolving dynamics of Bitcoin itself will shape the future of mining. The industry is seeing a trend towards more sustainable practices and decentralization of mining operations.

Conclusion

Bitcoin mining is a complex yet potentially rewarding process. It involves significant investment in hardware and electricity, along with a deep understanding of blockchain technology and mining principles. As the Bitcoin network grows and evolves, so too will the mining landscape, presenting new challenges and opportunities for those involved. Aspiring miners must thoroughly research and consider the economic, legal, and technological aspects of mining before embarking on this venture. With the right approach and resources, Bitcoin mining can not only be a lucrative endeavor but also a key contribution to the maintenance and security of the blockchain network.

POWERING THE FUTURE : BITCOIN MINNG

Mastering Ethereum Mining

Ethereum mining is an integral part of the Ethereum network, contributing to transaction processing, the creation of new Ether (ETH), and overall network security. Unlike Bitcoin mining, Ethereum mining was initially more accessible to the general public due to its resistance to specialized mining hardware. However, with the network's ongoing upgrades and shift towards Proof of Stake (PoS), the landscape is evolving. This guide provides an in-depth understanding of Ethereum mining, its processes, and considerations for those interested in engaging in mining activities.

Understanding Ethereum Mining

Ethereum mining involves solving complex mathematical puzzles to validate transactions and secure the network. Miners compete to complete transactions on the network by solving these puzzles, and the first one to solve the puzzle gets to add a new block to the Ethereum blockchain.

The Mining Process

1. **Transaction Compilation:** Miners collect a series of transactions from the Ethereum network's transaction pool.

2. **Proof of Work (PoW):** Ethereum, currently transitioning from PoW to PoS, requires miners to solve complex computational problems. In PoW, miners use their computational power to solve these puzzles.

3. **Creating a New Block:** The miner who first solves the puzzle creates a new block of transactions.

4. **Network Verification:** Other network participants then verify the block's validity.

5. **Reward:** The successful miner receives two types of rewards - a block reward and gas fees associated with the transactions in the block.

Equipment Required for Ethereum Mining

1. **Mining Hardware:** Ethereum mining started with CPUs and GPUs, but with increasing difficulty, more efficient hardware like ASIC miners are also being used.

2. **Mining Software:** Software is required to connect your mining hardware to the Ethereum network. Examples include Ethminer, Claymore, and PhoenixMiner.

3. **Adequate Cooling System:** Mining generates significant heat, requiring effective cooling solutions to maintain hardware efficiency.

4. **Reliable Internet Connection:** A stable and fast internet connection is crucial for continuous mining operations and staying synchronized with the Ethereum network.

Choosing a Mining Method

1. **Solo Mining:** Mining alone can be less efficient due to high competition and difficulty levels, but rewards are not shared.

2. **Mining Pools:** Joining a mining pool allows miners to combine computational power, increasing the chances of solving a block and earning rewards, which are shared among

pool members.

3. **Cloud Mining:** Renting mining power from companies with large mining farms is another option, though it typically offers lower returns and carries risks such as fraud.

Mining Difficulty and Profitability

Ethereum's mining difficulty adjusts dynamically, ensuring a consistent block time. Factors affecting profitability include electricity costs, hardware efficiency, network difficulty, and the price of ETH. It's crucial to calculate potential earnings versus expenses to determine the feasibility of mining.

Ethereum's Transition to Proof of Stake

Ethereum is transitioning to a Proof of Stake (PoS) model with its Ethereum 2.0 upgrade. PoS changes the way transactions are verified and blocks are added, eliminating the need for energy-intensive mining in favor of staking ETH to earn rewards. This shift will phase out traditional mining on the Ethereum network.

Legal and Regulatory Considerations

The legality of mining varies by country and jurisdiction. It's important for prospective miners to understand the legal landscape in their region, including tax implications and regulations regarding cryptocurrency mining.

Environmental Considerations

Ethereum mining, like other cryptocurrency mining activities, has been criticized for its environmental impact due to high energy consumption. The Ethereum 2.0 upgrade to PoS aims to significantly reduce this impact.

Preparing for Ethereum 2.0

With the transition to Ethereum 2.0, miners need to adapt. Options include shifting to mining other PoW cryptocurrencies, converting to Ethereum staking, or selling mining hardware.

Conclusion

Ethereum mining has been an exciting and potentially profitable activity, contributing significantly to the operation and security of the Ethereum network. However, with the upcoming Ethereum 2.0 upgrade and shift to PoS, the mining landscape is changing dramatically. Prospective miners should consider the current and future state of Ethereum, assess the profitability and feasibility of mining, and stay informed about the network's developments. While traditional mining on Ethereum may be phasing out, the network continues to offer opportunities for engagement and investment in the evolving world of cryptocurrencies.

A deep dive into Cloud Mining

Cloud mining has emerged as a popular alternative for individuals interested in cryptocurrency mining without the upfront investment in hardware and running costs. It allows users to rent mining capacity from remote data centers, making mining accessible to a wider audience. This comprehensive guide delves into the workings, advantages, risks, and considerations of cloud mining.

Understanding Cloud Mining

Cloud mining is a process that allows individuals to participate in cryptocurrency mining by renting processing power from remote data centers. These centers are equipped with specialized mining hardware and are typically located in areas with low electricity costs. Users can purchase a certain amount of 'hash power' and earn rewards proportional to their investment without directly handling any physical or software aspects of mining.

How Cloud Mining Works

1. **Choosing a Provider:** The first step is selecting a reputable cloud mining provider. This involves research to ensure legitimacy and assess profitability.

2. **Purchasing Hash Power:** Users buy a contract that provides them with a certain amount of hash power. The contract details the duration and the specific amount of power rented.

3. **Mining Operations:** The provider uses the collective power of all rented hardware to mine cryptocurrencies, typically Bitcoin, Ethereum, or other altcoins.

4. **Earning Rewards:** Rewards, usually in the form of mined cryptocurrency, are distributed to users based on the amount of hash power they rented.

Types of Cloud Mining

1. **Hosted Mining:** Rent physical mining hardware hosted by the service provider.

2. **Virtual Hosted Mining:** Rent a virtual private server and install your mining software.

3. **Leased Hashing Power:** Rent a certain amount of hashing power, without a dedicated physical or virtual computer. This is the most common form of cloud mining.

Advantages of Cloud Mining

1. **No Upfront Hardware Investment:** Eliminates the need for expensive mining equipment.

2. **Reduced Running Costs:** No worries about electricity costs, cooling systems, or maintenance.

3. **Simplicity and Convenience:** User-friendly, especially for those not technically inclined.

4. **Diversification:** Opportunity to mine different cryptocurrencies without additional hardware.

Choosing a Cloud Mining Provider

1. **Reputation:** Research the provider's history, user reviews, and community feedback.

2. **Contract Terms:** Understand contract duration, fees, and expected returns.

3. **Cryptocurrencies Offered:** Consider which cryptocurrencies you can mine and their potential profitability.

4. **Transparency:** Reliable providers offer regular updates about their mining farms and operations.

Risks and Considerations in Cloud Mining

1. **Scam Risk:** The cloud mining industry has been rife with scams. It's crucial to thoroughly vet providers.

2. **Lower Profits:** Due to operational costs and fees, cloud mining might offer lower returns compared to traditional mining.

3. **Market Volatility:** Cryptocurrency prices are volatile, which can significantly affect profitability.

4. **Loss of Control:** Dependence on the provider for mining operations means less control over your mining activity.

5. **Contractual Limitations:** Some contracts may have clauses that are not favorable in certain market conditions.

Profitability of Cloud Mining

Calculating the profitability of cloud mining involves considering the cost of the contract, the hash rate, the efficiency of the mining operation, the current price of the cryptocurrency, and the mining difficulty. Tools and calculators are available online to help estimate potential earnings.

Legal and Regulatory Aspects

Before engaging in cloud mining, it's important to be aware of the legal and regulatory environment in your country regarding cryptocurrency mining and earnings.

Environmental Considerations

Cloud mining centers, especially those using non-renewable energy sources, contribute to environmental concerns associated with cryptocurrency mining. Some providers have started using renewable energy sources to mitigate this impact.

The Future of Cloud Mining

As the cryptocurrency market evolves, cloud mining continues to adapt. Developments in renewable energy and blockchain technology could impact its sustainability and profitability.

Conclusion

Cloud mining offers an accessible entry point into cryptocurrency mining, eliminating the need for technical expertise and significant capital investment in hardware. However, it requires careful consideration of the provider's legitimacy, contract terms, and an understanding of the associated risks and market dynamics. While it presents an opportunity for passive income, prospective cloud miners should approach this venture with diligence, informed decision-making, and an awareness of the evolving landscape of cryptocurrency mining.

Chapter 3

Ensuring the Security of Your Crypto Wallet

In the digital age, securing a crypto wallet is as essential as safeguarding your physical wallet. Cryptocurrencies, being entirely digital, are subject to various online threats, including hacking, phishing, and fraud. This guide provides in-depth insights into securing your crypto wallet, ensuring your digital assets are well-protected.

Understanding Crypto Wallets

A crypto wallet is a digital tool that allows you to store, send, and receive cryptocurrencies like Bitcoin, Ethereum, and others. It contains private keys, secret codes that give you access to your cryptocurrencies, making wallet security paramount.

Types of Crypto Wallets

1. **Hot Wallets:** These are connected to the internet, providing convenience but are more vulnerable to online attacks. Examples include desktop, mobile, and web wallets.

2. **Cold Wallets:** These are offline wallets, more secure but less convenient for frequent transactions. Examples include hardware wallets and paper wallets.

Securing Your Crypto Wallet

1. **Use Strong and Unique Passwords:** Your wallet's first line of defense is a strong password. Use a complex combination of numbers, letters, and special characters. Avoid using the same password across different platforms.

2. **Enable Two-Factor Authentication (2FA):** 2FA adds an extra layer of security. Even if someone gets your password, they won't be able to access your wallet without the second factor, usually a code sent to your phone or email.

3. **Use Reputable Wallets:** Choose wallets with a strong reputation and positive user reviews. Reputable wallets have better security measures and regular updates.

4. **Keep Software Updated:** Regularly update your wallet software to ensure you have the latest security enhancements and bug fixes.

5. **Beware of Phishing Attacks:** Be cautious of emails or messages that ask for your wallet details. Always verify the sender's authenticity.

6. **Regular Backups:** Regularly backup your wallet, especially after every transaction. Store backups in multiple secure locations.

7. **Use Multi-Signature Features:** Some wallets offer multi-signature options, where multiple approvals are needed for a transaction. This is especially useful for business or joint account holders.

8. **Secure Your Private Keys:** Never share your private keys. Store them offline in a secure place, such as a safe deposit box or a secure home safe.

9. **Use Hardware Wallets for Large Amounts:** For substantial cryptocurrency holdings, use hardware wallets. They store your private keys offline, providing protection from online threats.

10. **Educate Yourself About Security Threats:** Stay informed about the latest security threats and how to protect against them.

Dealing with Exchanges

1. **Choose Secure Exchanges:** When buying or selling cryptocurrencies, use reputable and secure exchanges.
2. **Don't Store Large Amounts on Exchanges:** Exchanges are prime targets for hackers. Store only what you need for trading and transfer the rest to your secure wallet.

Understanding the Risks

1. **Hacking:** Despite security measures, wallets, especially hot wallets, are susceptible to hacking.
2. **Lost Access:** Losing access to your wallet, especially cold wallets, can mean losing your cryptocurrencies.
3. **Scams and Fraud:** The crypto world is full of scams. Be vigilant about where and to whom you send your cryptocurrencies.

Recovery Plans

1. **Seed Phrases:** Many wallets provide a seed phrase, a series of words that can be used to recover your wallet. Store this phrase securely and offline.
2. **Legacy Planning:** Ensure that trusted family members know how to access your wallet in case something happens to you.

The Human Element

1. **Be Cautious with Social Engineering:** Social engineering attacks are designed to trick you into revealing your wallet details. Be skeptical of unsolicited advice or help offers.
2. **Keep Your Holdings Private:** Avoid publicizing your cryptocurrency holdings to reduce the risk of being targeted.

Legal Considerations

1. **Regulatory Compliance:** Be aware of the legal and regulatory requirements related to cryptocurrency in your jurisdiction.
2. **Tax Implications:** Understand the tax implications of holding, trading, and transacting in cryptocurrencies.

Conclusion

Securing your crypto wallet involves a mix of technological measures, personal vigilance, and continuous learning. By employing strong passwords, enabling 2FA, using reputable wallets, being aware of online threats, and regularly backing up your wallet, you can significantly reduce the risks associated with digital asset storage. Remember, in the world of cryptocurrencies, the responsibility for security largely rests on the individual. Staying informed, cautious, and proactive is the key to safeguarding your digital wealth.

Chapter 4

Create your cryptocurrency : Basics

Cryptocurrency, a digital or virtual form of currency, has revolutionized the financial world since the advent of Bitcoin. With the rise in popularity of cryptocurrencies, many are intrigued by the prospect of creating their own. This comprehensive guide delves into the steps, considerations, and technological aspects involved in creating a cryptocurrency.

Understanding the Basics of Cryptocurrency

Before embarking on creating a cryptocurrency, it's essential to understand its foundational elements:

1. **Blockchain Technology:** Most cryptocurrencies operate on a blockchain, a decentralized ledger of all transactions across a network.

2. **Consensus Mechanisms:** This is the process used to achieve agreement on the state of the blockchain. Popular mechanisms include Proof of Work (PoW) and Proof of Stake (PoS).

3. **Smart Contracts:** These are self-executing contracts with the terms of the agreement directly written into code.

4. **Tokens vs. Coins:** Tokens operate on existing blockchains, while coins have their blockchain.

Step-by-Step Process to Create a Cryptocurrency

1. Define the Purpose of Your Cryptocurrency

Before creating a cryptocurrency, define its purpose. Is it for a specific online community, a decentralized application (dApp), or a broader transactional currency?

2. Choose Between a Coin or a Token

- **Creating a Coin:** This involves creating a new blockchain. It requires substantial technical knowledge and resources.
- **Creating a Token:** It's easier and involves creating a cryptocurrency on an existing blockchain, like Ethereum, which supports tokens with its ERC-20 standard.

3. Design the Blockchain (If Creating a Coin)

If you opt for a coin, you'll need to design and build a blockchain. Key considerations include:

- **Consensus Mechanism:** Choose between PoW, PoS, or other mechanisms.
- **Blockchain Architecture:** Decide on permissioned vs. permissionless blockchains.
- **Node Structure:** Define how the nodes will function within your blockchain.

4. Develop the Token (If Creating a Token)

Creating a token is simpler than a coin. Platforms like Ethereum, Binance Smart Chain, and others provide a template for token creation. You'll need to:

- **Select a Blockchain Platform:** Choose a platform that supports token creation.
- **Write the Smart Contract:** Code the rules, total supply, and other features of your

token.

5. Code Your Cryptocurrency

- **For a Coin:** This requires extensive coding knowledge or hiring developers. You'll need to code the blockchain protocol, consensus mechanism, and create the blockchain's software.
- **For a Token:** Use the blockchain platform's existing protocols and standards to create your token, typically with fewer coding requirements.

6. Test Your Cryptocurrency

Before launch, thoroughly test your cryptocurrency to ensure its security and functionality. This includes testing the blockchain (for coins), smart contracts, and transaction processes.

7. Launch the Cryptocurrency

Once testing is complete, launch your cryptocurrency. For coins, this means deploying your blockchain and its nodes. For tokens, it's about deploying your smart contract on the chosen platform.

8. Mining and Maintenance

For a new coin, establish the mining process. For both coins and tokens, ongoing maintenance is crucial to fix bugs, improve functionality, and adapt to changes in technology and demand.

9. Ensure Legal Compliance

Understand and adhere to the legal and regulatory requirements in jurisdictions you plan to operate.

10. Promote and Build a Community

Promotion and community building are critical. Engage with potential users and investors through social media, forums, and cryptocurrency communities.

Considerations for Creating a Cryptocurrency

1. **Technical Expertise:** Creating a coin requires in-depth technical knowledge, while tokens are less complex but still need basic coding skills.
2. **Security:** Implement robust security measures to protect against hacking and fraud.
3. **Scalability:** Design your cryptocurrency to handle a growing number of transactions.
4. **Interoperability:** Consider the ability of your cryptocurrency to interact with other blockchains and systems.
5. **Cost:** Factor in the cost of development, testing, launch, and ongoing maintenance.
6. **Adoption and Use Cases:** Focus on real-world applications and usability to drive adoption.

Advanced Considerations in Cryptocurrency Creation

1. **Tokenomics:** This involves defining the economics of your token, including supply, distribution, and how it's used within your ecosystem.
2. **Decentralization:** Decide the level of decentralization appropriate for your cryptocurrency.

3. **Governance:** Establish governance protocols for decision-making within your cryptocurrency network.

4. **Compliance with Regulations:** Keep abreast with changing regulations in the crypto space to ensure compliance.

5. **Community Involvement:** Engage with your community for feedback, governance, and promotion.

Challenges in Creating a Cryptocurrency

1. **Technical Challenges:** Developing a secure, efficient, and scalable cryptocurrency is technically challenging.

2. **Regulatory Hurdles:** Navigating the complex and evolving regulatory landscape is difficult.

3. **Market Competition:** Standing out in a crowded market requires a unique value proposition.

4. **Security Threats:** Protecting against cybersecurity threats is an ongoing concern.

The Future of Cryptocurrency Development

The cryptocurrency space is rapidly evolving, with advancements in blockchain technology, regulatory shifts, and changing market dynamics. Staying informed and adaptable is key to the success of any cryptocurrency project.

Conclusion

Creating a cryptocurrency is a complex but potentially rewarding endeavor that requires technical expertise, strategic planning, legal compliance, and community engagement. Whether opting to create a coin or a token, the process involves careful consideration of various technical, legal, and market factors. By following the steps outlined in this guide and staying abreast of the latest developments in the crypto space, you can embark on the journey of creating a cryptocurrency with a solid foundation for potential success.

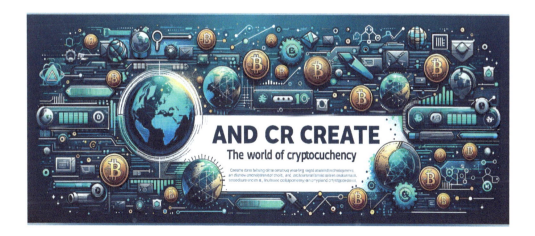

Chapter 5

Art of Cryptocurrency Trading : Basics

Trading cryptocurrencies can be a lucrative venture if done correctly. Here's a comprehensive guide on how to earn money through crypto trading, encapsulated in key points:

1. Understanding Cryptocurrency Markets

- **Market Dynamics**: Cryptocurrencies are known for their volatility, providing opportunities for high returns but also high risks.
- **Types of Cryptocurrencies**: Different cryptocurrencies like Bitcoin, Ethereum, and altcoins have unique characteristics and market behaviors.

2. Fundamental Analysis

- **Economic Indicators**: Assess the health of the cryptocurrency market through factors like market capitalization, the technology behind the currency, and the team.
- **News and Events**: Stay informed about global events, regulatory changes, and technological advancements that can impact prices.

3. Technical Analysis

- **Chart Patterns**: Learn to read and interpret price charts, identifying patterns that indicate potential market movements.
- **Indicators and Tools**: Utilize tools like moving averages, RSI, and Fibonacci retracements to make informed decisions.

4. Risk Management

- **Diversification**: Spread your investments across different cryptocurrencies to mitigate risk.
- **Stop-Loss Orders**: Use stop-loss orders to limit potential losses.

5. Trading Strategies

- **Day Trading**: Involves buying and selling on short-term movements within the market.
- **Swing Trading**: Capitalizes on trends in the market over days or weeks.
- **Scalping**: Profiting from small price gaps created by order flows or spread differences.
- **Position Trading**: Long-term approach based on fundamental analysis.

6. Leverage and Margin Trading

- **Understanding Leverage**: Leverage can amplify gains but also magnifies losses.
- **Margin Calls**: Be aware of the risks of margin calls, where you need to provide additional funds to maintain your position.

7. Using Exchanges and Wallets Safely

- **Choosing an Exchange**: Select exchanges based on security, fees, and ease of use.
- **Secure Storage**: Use a combination of hot and cold wallets for security.

8. Regulatory and Tax Compliance

- **Stay Informed**: Regulations can vary by country and change over time.
- **Tax Obligations**: Understand and comply with tax regulations regarding cryptocurrency gains.

9. Psychological Factors

- **Emotional Discipline**: Avoid emotional trading; decisions should be based on logic and analysis.
- **Fear of Missing Out (FOMO)**: Be wary of making impulsive decisions driven by FOMO.

10. Continuous Learning and Adaptation

- **Stay Updated**: The crypto market is constantly evolving. Keep learning and adapting to new tools and information.

11. Networking and Community Involvement

- **Join Communities**: Engage with other traders and enthusiasts to exchange information and strategies.

12. Realistic Expectations

- **No Guaranteed Profits**: Understand that profits are not guaranteed and there is always a risk of loss.

13. Experimentation and Practice

- **Demo Accounts**: Use demo accounts to practice trading without risking real money.
- **Small Investments**: Start with small investments to understand market dynamics.

14. Innovative Approaches

- **Algorithmic Trading**: Explore automated trading systems to execute trades based on predefined criteria.
- **Staying Ahead of Trends**: Keep an eye on emerging trends such as DeFi (Decentralized Finance) and NFTs (Non-Fungible Tokens).

15. Long-term Perspective

- **HODLing**: Some traders choose to "HODL" or hold their cryptocurrencies for a long-term gain.

Conclusion

Successful crypto trading requires a blend of knowledge, strategy, and emotional control. By understanding the market, employing robust analysis techniques, and practicing prudent risk .

Chapter 6
Crypto Trading Bot

Cryptocurrency trading bots are automated software that assist investors in making trading decisions and executing trades in the cryptocurrency market. These bots work based on a set of predefined rules and algorithms. Here's a detailed analysis of their benefits and drawbacks:

Benefits of Crypto Trading Bots

1. **Efficiency and Speed**: Bots can process data and execute trades much faster than humans, capitalizing on market opportunities instantly.

2. **Emotionless Trading**: Bots eliminate emotional decision-making, which can lead to impulsive or poor trading choices.

3. **24/7 Market Operation**: Crypto markets operate 24/7, and bots can trade round the clock without fatigue, unlike human traders.

4. **Backtesting**: Most trading bots allow backtesting, enabling traders to test their strategies against historical data before risking real money.

5. **Diversification**: Bots can manage several trading accounts and assets simultaneously, allowing for greater diversification.

6. **Consistency**: Bots maintain a consistent trading strategy, which is difficult for human traders due to emotional and psychological factors.

7. **Risk Management**: Automated systems can incorporate risk management rules, limiting potential losses.

8. **Complex Strategies Execution**: Bots can execute complex strategies that might be challenging to implement manually.

Drawbacks of Crypto Trading Bots

1. **Requires Monitoring**: Despite being automated, bots require regular monitoring to ensure smooth operation and to adjust strategies as per market changes.

2. **Security Risks**: Using bots involves cybersecurity risks, including the potential for hacking and unauthorized access to trading accounts and funds.

3. **Technical Knowledge Required**: Setting up and optimizing bots often requires a certain level of technical and trading knowledge.

4. **Limited Understanding of Market Conditions**: Bots may not understand nuanced market conditions and may not perform well in unexpected or extreme market events.

5. **Cost**: Some effective bots can be expensive, requiring subscription fees, which may reduce overall profitability.

6. **Dependency on Specific Exchanges**: Some bots may only work with specific exchanges, limiting trading options.

7. **Market Risk**: The volatile nature of the crypto market means that the effectiveness of a trading strategy can vary, and bots are not immune to this.

8. **Over-Optimization**: There's a risk of over-optimizing a bot for past market conditions, which may not be predictive of future market behavior.

9. **False Sense of Security**: Relying too heavily on bots can give traders a false sense of security, leading to complacency in monitoring and updating trading strategies.

10. **Regulatory Risks**: The evolving regulatory landscape for cryptocurrencies may impact bot trading strategies and their legality in certain jurisdictions.

Conclusion

Crypto trading bots can be powerful tools for traders, offering advantages in terms of speed, efficiency, and the ability to execute complex strategies. However, they are not a guaranteed path to profit and come with their own set of risks and limitations. Traders must consider these factors and have a clear understanding of how bots operate. Additionally, they should not completely rely on bots but instead use them as a tool in a broader, well-thought-out trading strategy. Regular monitoring, strategy adjustments, and staying informed about market and regulatory changes are essential for successful trading, whether using bots or trading manually.

Chapter 7

Discovering the Metaverse: A Comprehensive Guide

The Metaverse is a collective virtual shared space, created by the convergence of virtually enhanced physical reality, augmented reality (AR), and the internet. It's a space where users interact with a computer-generated environment and other users.

1. Understanding the Metaverse

- **Definition**: A vast online space merging VR, AR, and 2D internet.
- **Technologies Involved**: VR headsets, AR glasses, smart devices, and high-speed internet.
- **Historical Context**: Roots in science fiction; now becoming a reality due to technological advances.

2. Components of the Metaverse

- **Virtual Worlds**: Digital environments where users can play, work, and socialize.
- **Avatars**: Digital representations of users in the Metaverse.
- **Economy**: Virtual economies with cryptocurrencies and NFTs (Non-Fungible Tokens).
- **Interoperability**: The ability of various metaverse platforms to interact and exchange information and assets.

3. Experiencing the Metaverse

- **Accessing the Metaverse**: Requires internet access and, ideally, VR/AR hardware.
- **Navigating Virtual Worlds**: User interfaces vary but generally involve 3D navigation.
- **Social Interaction**: Platforms like VRChat and Second Life offer social experiences.
- **Gaming**: Games like Fortnite and Roblox offer early forms of metaverse experiences.

4. Economic Aspects

- **Virtual Goods**: Trading and investing in digital assets.
- **Real Estate**: Buying and selling virtual land in platforms like Decentraland.
- **Employment Opportunities**: Jobs in virtual event management, content creation, etc.

5. The Role of Blockchain and Cryptocurrencies

- **Blockchain**: Ensures security and transparency in transactions.
- **Cryptocurrencies**: Used for transactions within the Metaverse.
- **NFTs**: Represent ownership of unique digital items.

6. Opportunities in the Metaverse

- **Business and Marketing**: New avenues for branding and e-commerce.

- **Education and Training**: Interactive learning environments.
- **Entertainment**: Concerts, exhibitions, and events in virtual settings.

7. Privacy and Security Concerns

- **Data Privacy**: Personal data management is crucial.
- **Security Risks**: Potential for cyber threats and how to mitigate them.

8. Ethical and Societal Implications

- **Social Impact**: Effects on human interaction and societal norms.
- **Digital Divide**: Access disparity among different socioeconomic groups.

9. The Future of the Metaverse

- **Predictions and Trends**: Expansion of VR/AR, integration with AI, and more immersive experiences.
- **Challenges Ahead**: Technical, ethical, and regulatory challenges.

10. How to Get Involved

- **Choosing a Platform**: Research and select based on interests (e.g., gaming, socializing, business).
- **Building a Presence**: Creating avatars, acquiring digital assets, and participating in communities.

11. Potential Risks and How to Navigate Them

- **Addiction**: Balancing virtual and real life.
- **Financial Risks**: Managing investments in digital assets.

12. Key Players in the Metaverse

- **Tech Giants**: Facebook (Meta), Google, Microsoft, and their roles.
- **Emerging Companies**: Smaller companies innovating in this space.

13. Building for the Metaverse

- **Development Tools**: Unity, Unreal Engine, etc.
- **Creating Content**: 3D modeling, coding, and creative writing.

14. Legal and Regulatory Aspects

- **Intellectual Property**: Managing rights in digital creations.
- **Regulation**: Current and potential government regulations.

15. Community and Culture

- **Online Communities**: Forums, social media groups, and events.
- **Cultural Impact**: How the metaverse is influencing popular culture.

Chapter 8
NFTs: Creating and Earning Money

Introduction to NFTs

- **Definition**: Non-Fungible Tokens (NFTs) are unique digital assets verified using blockchain technology, representing ownership of a specific item or piece of content.
- **Popularity**: Gained immense popularity as a way to buy, sell, and collect digital art and other virtual goods.

1. Understanding NFTs

- **Blockchain Technology**: NFTs are built on blockchain networks like Ethereum, ensuring authenticity and ownership.
- **Uniqueness and Rarity**: Each NFT is distinct, which can drive value.

2. The Market for NFTs

- **Scope**: Includes digital art, music, games, and virtual real estate.
- **Market Dynamics**: Influenced by demand, rarity, artist reputation, and community.

3. Creating NFTs

- **Choosing a Medium**: Digital art, photography, music, or any digital content.
- **Creating Digital Art**: Tools like Adobe Photoshop, Illustrator, or 3D software.
- **Minting Process**: Turning digital art into an NFT on a blockchain platform.

4. Selecting a Blockchain Platform

- **Ethereum**: Most popular for NFTs, offers robustness but higher transaction fees.
- **Other Blockchains**: Binance Smart Chain, Flow by Dapper Labs, Tezos, and others offer lower fees and energy efficiency.

5. Choosing an NFT Marketplace

- **Popular Platforms**: OpenSea, Rarible, Foundation, and others.
- **Fees and Features**: Consider listing fees, royalties, and user base.

6. Minting Your NFT

- **Process Overview**: Create a digital wallet, buy cryptocurrency, connect to an NFT platform, upload your artwork, and set sale details.
- **Gas Fees**: Costs associated with transactions on the blockchain.
- **Setting a Price**: Fixed price or auction; consider the rarity and potential demand.

7. Marketing Your NFT

- **Building a Brand**: Develop a unique style or theme.

- **Social Media Promotion**: Leverage platforms like Twitter, Instagram, and Discord.
- **Engaging with Communities**: Participate in NFT and art communities online.

8. Earning Money from NFTs

- **Direct Sales**: Earning from initial sales of your NFTs.
- **Royalties**: Earning a percentage from future resales.
- **Collaborations and Commissions**: Partner with brands or individuals.

9. Legal and Ethical Considerations

- **Copyright and Intellectual Property**: Ensure you have rights to the content you're minting.
- **Avoiding Plagiarism**: Originality is key in the NFT world.

10. Investing in NFTs

- **Buying NFTs**: Investing in other artists' NFTs as collector items.
- **Market Research**: Understanding trends and valuations in the NFT market.

11. Risks and Challenges

- **Market Volatility**: NFT market can be unpredictable.
- **Cybersecurity**: Protect your digital wallet and assets from theft.
- **Environmental Concerns**: Energy usage of blockchain transactions.

12. The Future of NFTs

- **Evolving Use Cases**: Beyond art, into realms like virtual real estate, gaming, and identity verification.
- **Integration with VR and AR**: Enhancing the experience of NFTs in virtual and augmented reality.

13. Tips for Success

- **Stay Informed**: Keep up with NFT and blockchain technology trends.
- **Networking**: Engage with other creators and collectors.
- **Innovation**: Continuously evolve your style and approach.

14. Case Studies

- **Successful NFT Artists**: Learn from those who have effectively navigated the market.
- **Market Analyses**: Understand what makes certain NFTs valuable.

15. Conclusion

Creating and earning money from NFTs is a blend of artistic creativity, technical know-how, and market understanding. While it offers unique opportunities for artists and creators, it's important to approach with a clear strategy, awareness of risks, and a commitment to ongoing learning and adaptation in this rapidly evolving space.

Chapter 9

The Future of Cryptocurrencies: Trends and Predictions

Cryptocurrencies have transformed the financial landscape, offering a decentralized, digital form of currency. Their future is a subject of much speculation and interest.

1. Growth and Mainstream Adoption

- **Increasing Acceptance**: More businesses and financial institutions are beginning to accept cryptocurrencies as payment.
- **Retail and E-commerce**: A rise in cryptocurrencies being used for everyday transactions.

2. Regulatory Landscape

- **Global Regulations**: Governments and financial authorities are working to develop regulations to manage the use and trading of cryptocurrencies.
- **Impact of Regulations**: Stricter regulations could impact the volatility and growth of cryptocurrencies.

3. Technological Advancements

- **Blockchain Evolution**: Continuous improvement in blockchain technology for enhanced security and efficiency.
- **Interoperability**: Focus on making different blockchain networks work together seamlessly.

4. Decentralized Finance (DeFi)

- **Growth of DeFi**: Expansion of decentralized financial services, challenging traditional banking.
- **Financial Inclusion**: DeFi could offer financial services to unbanked populations.

5. Cryptocurrency as an Investment

- **Institutional Investment:** More institutional investors are considering cryptocurrencies as a legitimate asset class.
- **Volatility and Speculation:** Cryptocurrency markets are known for their high volatility, which can attract speculators.

6. Digital Currencies and Central Banks

- **Central Bank Digital Currencies (CBDCs):** Countries may launch their digital currencies, impacting the crypto space.
- **Impact on Existing Cryptocurrencies:** Interaction between CBDCs and existing cryptocurrencies could shape the market.

7. Security and Cyber Risks

- **Enhanced Security Measures:** As the value and use of cryptocurrencies grow, so does the need for robust security solutions.
- **Risks of Hacks and Frauds:** Persistent threat to exchanges and wallets.

8. The Role of Cryptocurrencies in Emerging Economies

- **Remittances:** Easier and cheaper cross-border transactions.
- **Hyperinflation Hedge:** Cryptocurrencies can offer stability in countries with volatile economies.

9. Innovation in Cryptocurrency Use Cases

- **NFTs and Tokenization:** Expansion in non-fungible tokens (NFTs) and tokenization of assets.
- **Smart Contracts:** Broader application of smart contracts in various sectors.

10. Environmental Concerns and Solutions

- **Energy Consumption:** High energy usage of some cryptocurrencies, especially Bitcoin.
- **Sustainable Practices:** Shift towards more energy-efficient consensus mechanisms like Proof of Stake.

11. The Role of Cryptocurrencies in the Global Economy

- **Global Financial System:** Potential to become an integral part of the global financial system.
- **Economic Empowerment:** Offering financial empowerment and autonomy to individuals worldwide.

12. Market Integration and Financial Products

- **Crypto-based Financial Products:** Increase in products like crypto ETFs, futures, and derivatives.
- **Integration with Traditional Finance:** Cryptocurrencies becoming more integrated with traditional financial systems.

13. User Experience and Accessibility

- **Improvements in User Interface:** Making crypto platforms more user-friendly.
- **Wider Accessibility:** Efforts to make cryptocurrencies accessible to a broader audience.

14. Challenges and Concerns

- **Regulatory Uncertainty:** Ongoing uncertainty around regulations.
- **Market Stability:** Concerns about market bubbles and potential crashes.

15. The Potential of Cryptocurrencies

- **Disruptive Potential:** Cryptocurrencies have the potential to disrupt traditional finance.

- **Long-term Viability**: Assessing whether cryptocurrencies can sustain their growth and utility in the long term.

Conclusion

The future of cryptocurrencies is marked by both exciting opportunities and significant challenges. They hold the potential to revolutionize various aspects of finance and society, but this potential comes with a need for responsible innovation, robust security, and thoughtful regulation. As the world increasingly embraces digital technology, the role of cryptocurrencies is likely to become more pronounced, influencing economies and financial practices worldwide.

Trading skills : Improve your crypto trading process
In addition to chapters 5 and 6

Crypto trading involves buying and selling cryptocurrencies in the digital currency market. This market is known for its high volatility, presenting both opportunities and risks. Developing key skills is crucial for success in this arena.

1. Understanding Cryptocurrencies and Blockchain

- **Foundational Knowledge**: Learn the basics of cryptocurrencies and how blockchain technology works.
- **Different Cryptocurrencies**: Study different types of cryptocurrencies, their use cases, and technology.

2. Market Analysis Skills

- **Technical Analysis**: Learn to read charts and use technical indicators like RSI, MACD, and moving averages.
- **Fundamental Analysis**: Evaluate the intrinsic value of a cryptocurrency based on news, tech developments, and market trends.

3. Risk Management

- **Diversification**: Spread your investments across various assets to reduce risk.
- **Stop Loss and Take Profit**: Set these orders to automatically close trades at predetermined levels to manage losses and lock in profits.

4. Trading Strategies

- **Day Trading**: Buying and selling assets within a single trading day.
- **Swing Trading**: Holding assets for several days to capitalize on expected upward or downward market shifts.
- **Scalping**: Making numerous trades for small profits over very short periods.

5. Emotional Control

- **Avoid Emotional Decisions**: Don't let fear or greed drive your trading decisions.
- **Stress Management**: Develop techniques to manage stress effectively.

6. Continuous Learning

- **Stay Updated**: Keep abreast of the latest market news and trends.
- **Learning Resources**: Utilize books, courses, and seminars to deepen your understanding.

7. Utilizing Technology

- **Trading Platforms**: Familiarize yourself with various trading platforms and tools.
- **Crypto Trading Bots**: Understand how bots can automate trading based on specific algorithms.

8. Understanding and Adapting to Market Volatility

- **Volatility Nature**: Recognize that crypto markets are highly volatile.
- **Adapting Strategies**: Be flexible and adapt your strategies to changing market conditions.

9. Security Knowledge

- **Secure Transactions**: Learn about securing your cryptocurrency transactions.
- **Wallet Safety**: Understand the different types of wallets and how to keep them secure.

10. Networking and Community Engagement

- **Join Crypto Communities**: Engage with other traders and enthusiasts for insights and support.
- **Social Media and Forums**: Follow influencers and join discussions on platforms like Reddit and Twitter.

11. Legal and Regulatory Compliance

- **Stay Informed**: Keep up to date with the changing legal and regulatory landscape of cryptocurrencies.

12. Record Keeping and Tax Compliance

- **Record Transactions**: Keep detailed records of your transactions for tax purposes.
- **Understand Tax Obligations**: Be aware of how cryptocurrency trading impacts your taxes.

13. Patience and Long-term Perspective

- **Long-term Approach**: Understand that significant profits in crypto trading might require a long-term perspective.

14. Personal Finance Management

- **Invest Responsibly**: Only invest what you can afford to lose.
- **Budgeting**: Manage your finances effectively to support your trading activities.

15. Building a Trading Plan

- **Set Clear Goals**: Define what you want to achieve with your trading.
- **Develop a Strategy**: Create a trading plan that suits your goals, risk tolerance, and style.

Money Management in Crypto Trading: Balancing Risk and Reward

Money management in crypto trading is a critical skill that involves the effective handling of investment capital to maximize profits while minimizing risks. Given the volatile nature of cryptocurrencies, it's essential to have a robust strategy.

1. Understanding the Importance of Money Management

- **Fundamental Aspect:** It's the cornerstone of successful trading, crucial for both beginners and experienced traders.
- **Risk Mitigation:** Helps in protecting traders from significant losses during market downturns.

2. Setting Up a Trading Budget

- **Investment Capital:** Only use money that you can afford to lose. Avoid using essential funds like retirement savings.
- **Allocation:** Determine how much capital you will allocate to each trade.

3. Risk Management

- **Risk per Trade:** Limit the risk on each trade to a small percentage of your total capital, typically 1-2%.
- **Total Exposure:** Keep track of your total exposure in the market.

4. Diversification

- **Variety of Assets:** Spread your investments across different cryptocurrencies to mitigate risk.
- **Avoid Overconcentration:** Don't put all your capital into a single cryptocurrency.

5. Understanding Leverage and Margin Trading

- **High Risk, High Reward:** Leverage can amplify gains but also magnify losses.
- **Caution:** Use leverage cautiously, understanding the risks involved.

6. Using Stop Losses and Take Profit Orders

- **Stop Losses:** Set a stop loss to automatically sell an asset when it reaches a certain price to limit losses.
- **Take Profit:** Set a take profit order to secure profits when the price reaches your target.

7. The Psychology of Trading

- **Emotional Discipline:** Avoid letting emotions drive your trading decisions.
- **Avoiding Greed and Fear:** Don't let fear of missing out drive you to make risky trades or greed to keep you from taking profits.

8. Recording and Reviewing Trades

- **Trade Journal**: Keep a record of all your trades, including the rationale for each trade.
- **Reviewing**: Regularly review your trades to learn from successes and mistakes.

9. Adapting to Market Changes

- **Flexibility**: Be willing to adjust your strategy in response to market changes.
- **Staying Informed**: Keep up to date with the latest market trends and news.

10. The Role of Research

- **Informed Decisions**: Base your trading decisions on thorough research rather than speculation.
- **Continuous Learning**: Stay educated about new developments in the crypto space.

11. Long-Term vs. Short-Term Trading

- **Different Strategies**: Understand the differences between long-term holding and short-term trading.
- **Risk and Reward**: Recognize that different strategies have different risk profiles.

12. Understanding and Using Technical Analysis

- **Market Trends**: Use technical analysis to understand market trends.
- **Indicators and Charts**: Learn to use various indicators and chart patterns.

13. Money Management Tools

- **Trading Bots and Software**: Consider using automated tools to help manage trades.
- **Budgeting Tools**: Use budgeting tools to keep track of your finances.

14. Dealing with Losses

- **Inevitability of Losses**: Accept that losses are part of trading.
- **Learning from Losses**: Use losses as an opportunity to learn and improve.

15. Developing a Personalized Money Management Plan

- **Personal Risk Tolerance**: Tailor your money management strategy to your personal risk tolerance and trading style.
- **Goals and Objectives**: Align your trading approach with your financial goals.

Conclusion

Effective money management in crypto trading is about balancing the potential for high returns with the risk of significant losses. It involves careful planning, discipline, and continuous learning. By implementing sound money management practices, traders can navigate the volatile crypto markets more effectively, making informed decisions that align with their long-term financial objectives.

Utilizing Crypto Bots in Trading: Evaluating the Pros and Cons

The use of automated trading bots in the cryptocurrency market is a topic of much debate. These bots are programmed to execute trades based on specific algorithms and criteria. Understanding the advantages and disadvantages is essential for making an informed decision.

Advantages of Using Crypto Trading Bots

1. **Efficiency and Speed**: Bots can process and execute trades faster than humans, taking advantage of market opportunities almost instantaneously.
2. **Emotionless Trading**: Bots eliminate emotional biases, making decisions based purely on data and pre-set criteria, avoiding emotional trading mistakes like fear or greed.
3. **Market Availability**: Cryptocurrency markets operate 24/7, and bots can trade continuously, ensuring no missed opportunities.
4. **Backtesting Opportunities**: Many bots offer the ability to test trading strategies against historical market data, providing insights into their potential effectiveness.
5. **Consistency in Trading**: Unlike humans, bots can maintain a consistent trading strategy without being influenced by external factors like fatigue or distractions.
6. **Diversification**: Bots can handle multiple cryptocurrencies and strategies simultaneously, spreading risk.

Disadvantages of Using Crypto Trading Bots

1. **Complex Setup and Maintenance**: Setting up and maintaining a trading bot can be complex, often requiring programming knowledge and continuous tweaking.
2. **Security Risks**: Bots involve sharing your API keys with third-party services, which can be a security risk if not managed properly.
3. **Market Unpredictability**: Bots follow pre-set rules and may not adapt well to sudden market changes or unusual events.
4. **Costs**: Effective bots can be expensive, and there are additional costs like subscription fees and the cost of trading.
5. **Over-reliance on Automation**: There's a risk of becoming too reliant on bots, neglecting the importance of human oversight and decision-making.
6. **Regulatory Risks**: The regulatory environment for cryptocurrencies is still evolving, and using bots might be affected by future regulatory changes.

Considerations for Using Crypto Trading Bots

1. **Understanding Your Needs**: Assess whether a trading bot suits your trading style, risk tolerance, and technical expertise.
2. **Choosing the Right Bot**: Research and select a bot that aligns with your specific strategy and has a proven track record.
3. **Ongoing Monitoring**: Regularly monitor and adjust the bot's settings in response to market conditions.

4. **Combining Human and Bot Trading**: Consider using bots for certain repetitive tasks while keeping strategic decisions in human hands.

5. **Learning and Adapting**: Keep learning about market trends and adapt your strategies accordingly.

Ethical and Practical Implications

1. **Fairness in Trading**: The use of bots raises questions about fairness, especially when considering traders without access to advanced technology.

2. **Market Impact**: Widespread use of bots could potentially lead to market manipulation concerns.

Conclusion

Using crypto trading bots can be both a good and bad idea, depending on individual circumstances. The key lies in understanding both the benefits and drawbacks, aligning bot use with personal trading goals, and maintaining an active role in managing and overseeing automated strategies. While bots offer efficiency and consistency, they cannot entirely replace human insight and adaptability, especially in a market as volatile and unpredictable as cryptocurrency. Therefore, a balanced approach, combining the strengths of both automated and manual trading, might be the most prudent path for many traders.

Conclusion: Navigating the World of Cryptocurrencies

In summary, the realm of cryptocurrencies represents a dynamic and transformative sector, reflecting the fusion of technology and finance. As we've explored in this guide, cryptocurrencies are much more than just digital assets; they embody a new era of decentralized finance, offering both challenges and opportunities.

The key to successfully navigating this landscape lies in understanding the intricacies of blockchain technology, the mechanics of various cryptocurrencies, and the market forces that drive their value. The rise of platforms for trading, investing, and even creating digital currencies and assets like NFTs (Non-Fungible Tokens) underscores the ever-expanding scope of this domain.

However, with innovation comes responsibility. It's imperative for users, investors, and enthusiasts to remain vigilant about the associated risks, such as market volatility, regulatory changes, and security threats. Staying informed and educated is crucial in making prudent decisions.

Looking ahead, the future of cryptocurrencies seems poised for continued evolution. From potential mainstream adoption and the impact of emerging technologies like DeFi (Decentralized Finance) to the ongoing debates surrounding regulation and ethical implications, the journey of cryptocurrencies is far from reaching its zenith.

In essence, the cryptocurrency guide serves as a compass in a vast digital ocean, offering insights and directions but also reminding us of the need for cautious navigation. As we embrace this digital revolution, let us approach it with a balanced blend of enthusiasm and discernment, ready to explore the myriad possibilities that lie ahead in the world of cryptocurrencies.

Thanks for reading and don't forget to leave review on Amazon, that could be help us. Thank you

Other E-book available by the same author

Metavers : How to invest ?

www.ingramcontent.com/pod-product-compliance
Lightning Source LLC
Chambersburg PA
CBHW041155050326
40690CB00004B/575